MAJOR

Luck Zytowski

MAJOR by Luck Zytowski

Copyright © 2021 Luck Zytowski

All rights reserved.

Published by Luck Zytowski

Manassas, VA, United States of America

luckzytowski@gmail.com
beckluzy.wordpress.com

No parts of this publication may be reproduced, stored in a retrieval system, or transmitted in any form or by any means, electronic, mechanical, photocopying, recording, or otherwise, without the prior written permission of the copyright owner.

This book is sold subject to the condition that it shall not, by way of trade or otherwise, be lent, resold, hired out, or otherwise circulated without the publisher's prior consent in any form of binding or cover other than that in which it is published and without a similar condition including this condition being imposed on the subsequent purchaser. Under no circumstances may any part of this book be photocopied for resale.

ISBN: 978-0-578-30412-0

To those of us who made it

and to those who didn't.

Trigger Warning

eating disorder,
sexual assault,
& self harm.

CONTENTS

II	THE HIGH PRIESTESS
III	THE EMPRESS
O	THE FOOL
IV	THE EMPEROR
VI	THE LOVERS
V	THE HIEROPHANT
IX	THE HERMIT
VIII	STRENGTH
XII	THE HANGED MAN
XVIII	THE MOON
XVII	THE STAR
XI	JUSTICE
XVI	THE TOWER
XV	THE DEVIL
I	THE MAGICIAN
XX	JUDGEMENT
XIX	THE SUN
XIV	TEMPERANCE
XIII	DEATH
VII	THE CHARIOT
X	WHEEL OF FORTUNE
XXI	THE WORLD

What if you could take the important parts
that make up who you are
and lay them out in front of you?

Shuffle the deck, spread them out, and try
to understand yourself.

Feel those bursts of emotion, uncontrollable
events that dictate how your personality
changes and fluctuates through your life.

Major and minor.

Each piece creates a full deck.
Without one, the deck is incomplete.
You are incomplete.

Pull out cards and connect the
Major pieces of myself to you.

Flip until you feel like stopping.

Rip the pages out and
shuffle them yourself.

THE HIGH PRIESTESS

The chair isn't as comfortable as I'd hoped. When you picture going to a therapist, there's almost always a couch. The chair is sturdy below me, my shoulders slump over in hopes of making me smaller. I hear the clack of their nails on the keyboard each time I answer one of their questions. I'm usually the one that listens to people's problems, not vomit them out. My face flushes and I hang my head every time I get out a word. Nothing I've gone through ever seems as bad when it's out in the open. *I don't deserve to be here.* I automatically snort at the voice. The entire reason I'm here. My therapist picks up on it and suddenly, the voice isn't only in my head. It's on display and just as vulnerable as me. Something within me loosens. My back lies further into the chair, my legs spreading out lazily. Maybe it isn't as uncomfortable as I'd thought.

II

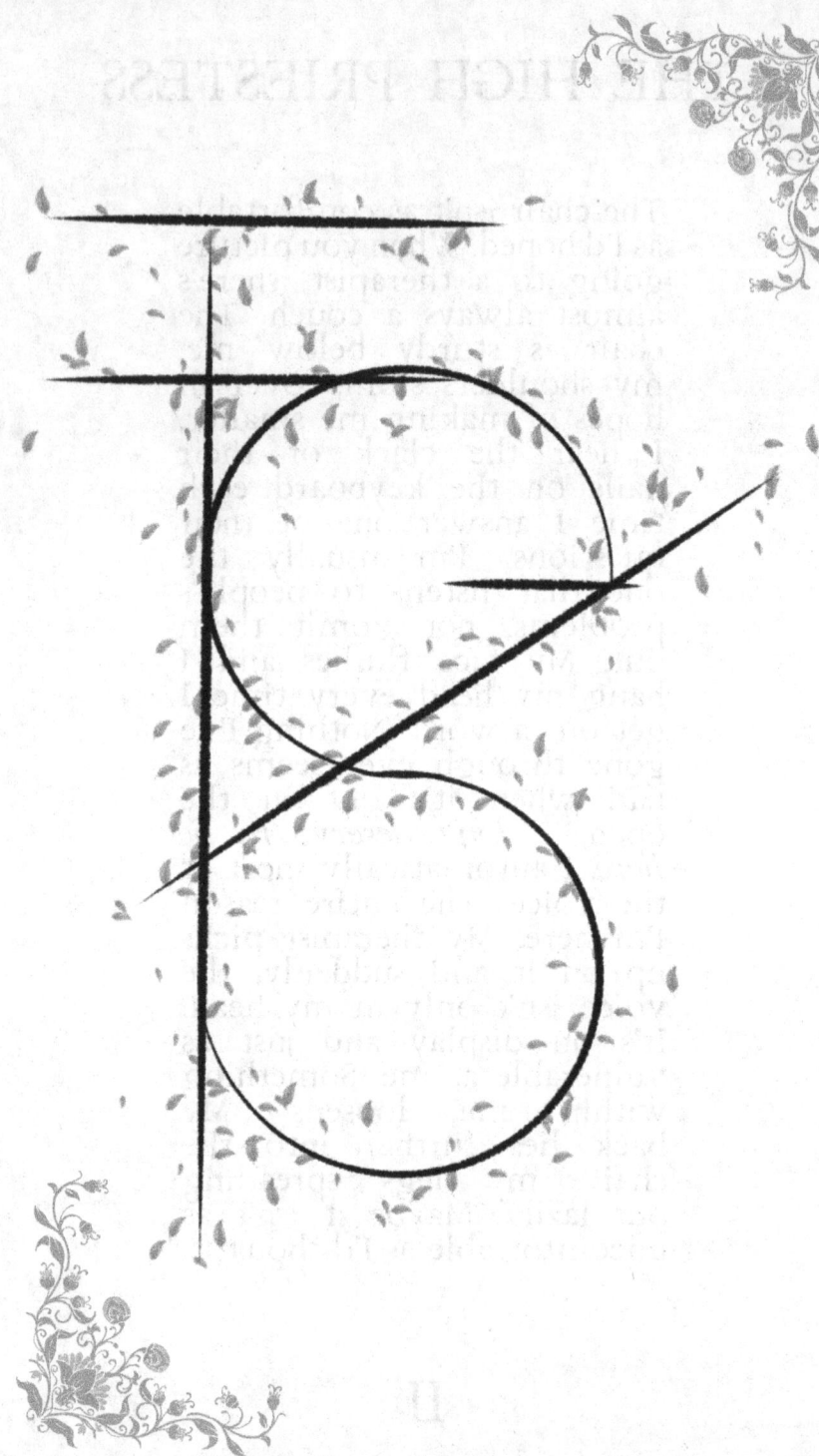

THE EMPRESS

I'll always be my mother's baby girl, even when I tell her I'm neither of those things. My bark has gotten rough from her ignorance, saving the soft heartwood inside. In all her pruning and shaping of my branches above, my roots have flourished in the depths below. Bits of them peek out of the ground as I reach new distances of separation. I can feel her on the sidelines, always ready to trim the excess I have grown while away and get me back to the perfect shape. At my age, she was as skinny as a twig. While I could snap just as easily, she reminds me of the chubbiness hugging my stomach. I didn't realize at first, I need that to survive, that thin layer of fat so my organs don't spill out like the vomit splashing into the toilet. She encourages me to take shots before I'm even 21. The apple cider vinegar still burns the back of my throat.

III

III

THE FOOL

My bark was once as strong as white oak, keeping at bay the fiercest of flames. But the phoenix that nested in the hollow of my chest has left its home as tinder. The charred remains of a skeletal structure whose roots have been torn from the fertile ground it was once in. They left a hatchling buried in their ashes. The hatchling tries to hide from the outside, they don't want to be burned before they can even learn to fly, but its predecessor has burned the foliage I was once flush with. I know the only way to salvation is to take this life and find new soil to sink my roots into. To create a new home is to also create a tinder for another to strike once more. I could be a fool, but there's one way to find out. I put myself on display in exchange for the chance at new growth. An old friend leads me to the land of misfits and the flutter of the hatchling's wings matches the wobble in my voice.

O

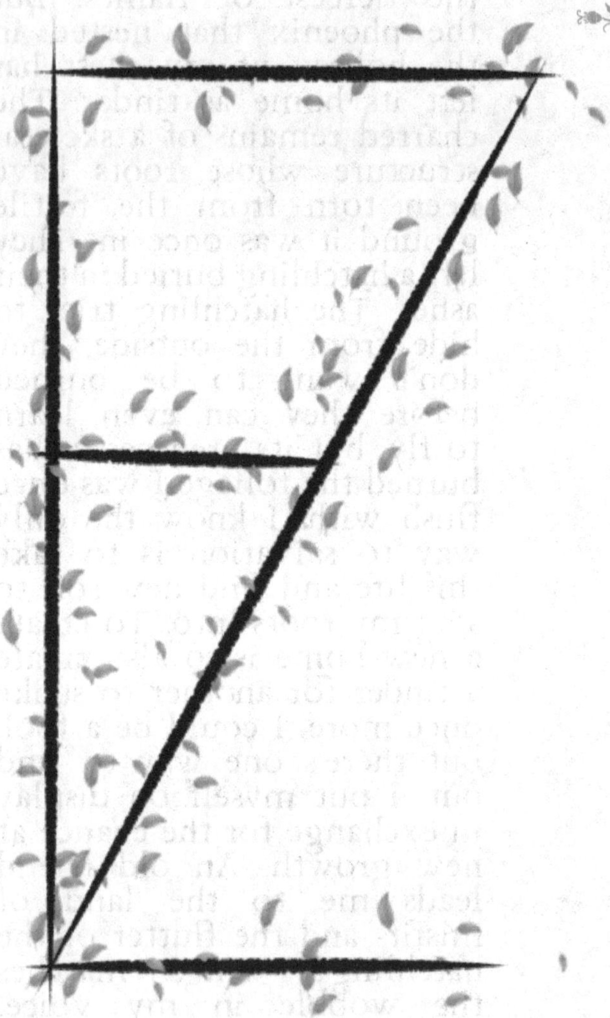

THE EMPEROR

I remember the hole in the wall of my childhood bedroom. I can't remember what I did that caused my father to slam the door open hard enough. He patched it up the next day and sat me down to talk. I've learned to stay silent, no use in fighting when they won't listen. My stance is steady, and his speech bounces off the thick bark I've grown. There's a comfort in the shade he brings, towering over me and my brothers. It's colder without the sun. As I grow, I feel myself reaching farther and farther out of the shade and feel the heat as my petals stretch open. His little princess. His baby girl. I flinch at the warm words. How do I break the news that his daughter is dead? In her place stands a child with those same memories, hoping he'll accept me as I show off the new foliage I've grown out the world. I want to be able to rest under the shade when the sun burns my skin and I have nowhere else to go. Relaxing in the old comfort, nervous to make the wrong move.

IV

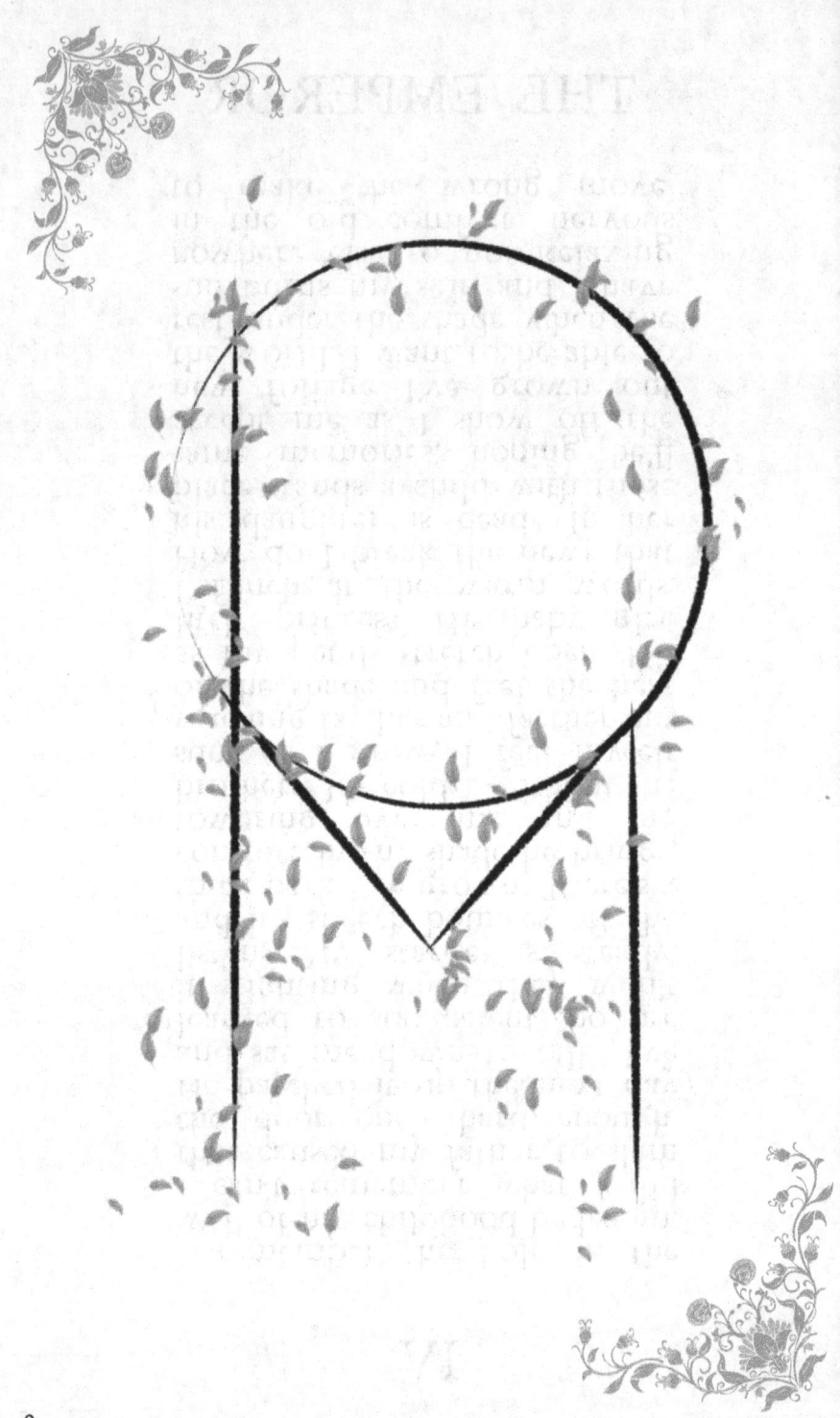

THE LOVERS

We've had some trials and tribulations they and I. Couldn't be together but couldn't seem to stay apart. So alike in all but perspective. I remember when they said I reminded them of themselves when they were younger. I wasn't sure how to take that. I'm still not. Maybe they're a little vain. The beginning happened in such a rush the leaves had barely touched the ground when it ended the first time. It came with so much pain and confusion, but I wouldn't change it. The warmth I feel when they smile in my direction, that soft look in their eyes, is something I never want to be rid of. Our roots twist together as they tackle me onto the bed, their laughter like birdsong. For a moment, my stress flies off in the wind. Being with them feels so natural now it scares me. I've had too many people in my life come and go. Pluck an apple or two and then continue on. They always ask me why I stare. To remember.

VI

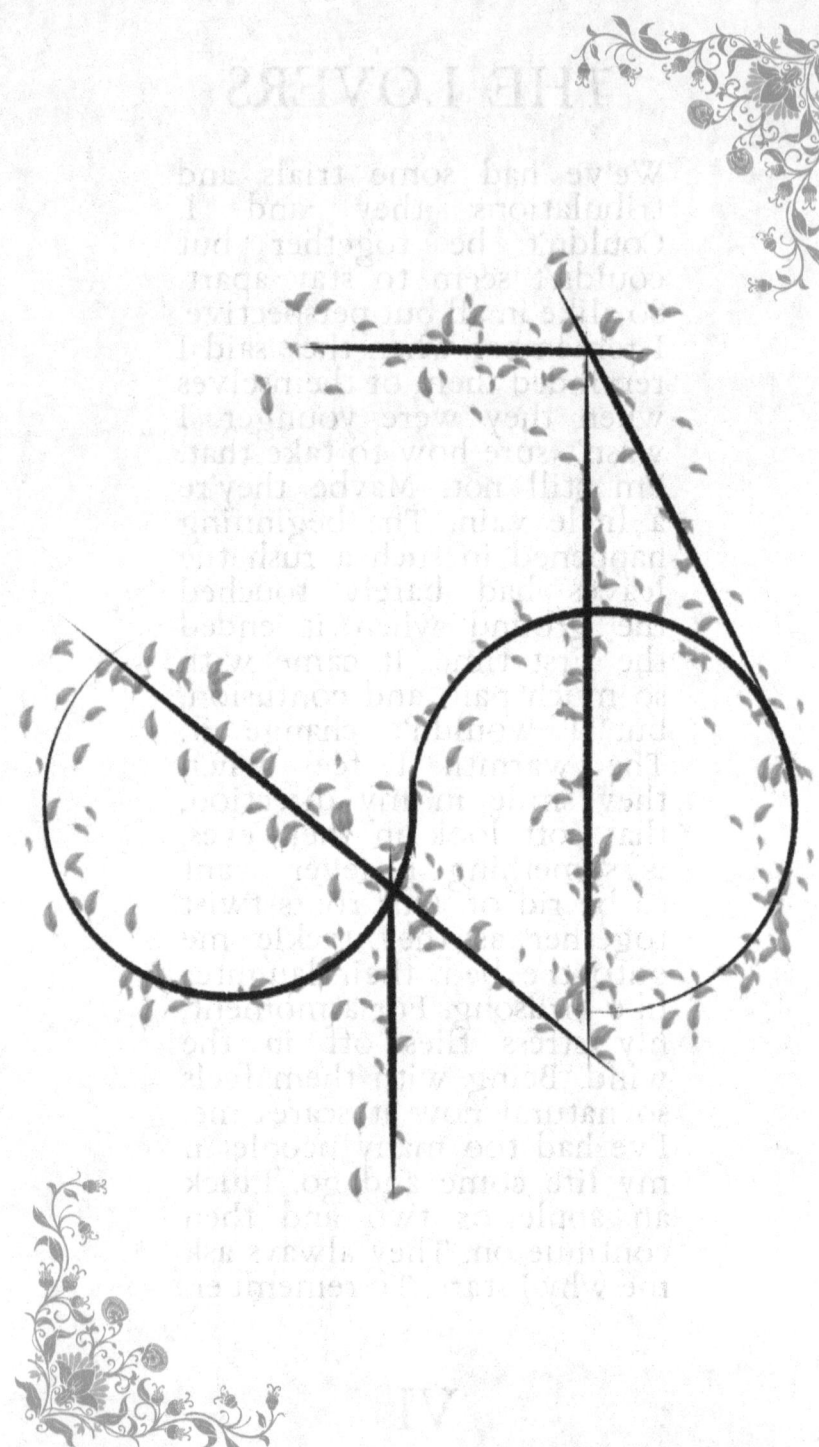

THE HIEROPHANT

The guilt I feel when I enter a church is embedded into my being. How is it I feel more beneath the skin of a tree than the skin of the savior on my tongue? The energy of the Earth as I root my feet to the ground is more than I've felt down on my knees before your son who hangs from the rafters, his death immortalized. I come to wonder how he would feel to see so many statues of him today. As I stand by to my devout parents I think of my altar, placed thoughtfully at home where my private spirituality resides. It's hidden behind unanswered questions and quickly packed away candles before anyone comes in. Some of your followers would burn me for my solitary practice, saying I'm blasphemous when all I do is believe differently. All I want is to understand. The universe and I. To become connected to the world around me as well as the world of the divine. To take my fate into my own hands, not to depend on someone who has never answered me.

V

THE HIEROPHANT

THE HERMIT

Stay home. Stay in your head. Travel farther than you've ever gone before without stepping on solid ground. All the time in the world crumbles in your periphery. Sit with your shadow and understand why it follows you. It's just as much a part of you as the heart that beats in your chest. If you ignore it forever, it'll only get bigger until that's all anyone can see. Stretch muscles you've never used before and feel your arms and legs wobble as you balance precariously on one leg. The shaking means you're doing something right. Feel the center of your body as you search for the center of your mind. Your knowledge of herbs and their properties grows immensely in just a few days. You tell your family it's for tea purposes and you aren't technically lying. Whether they're in a mug or a jar they can still get the job done with the right intent.

IX

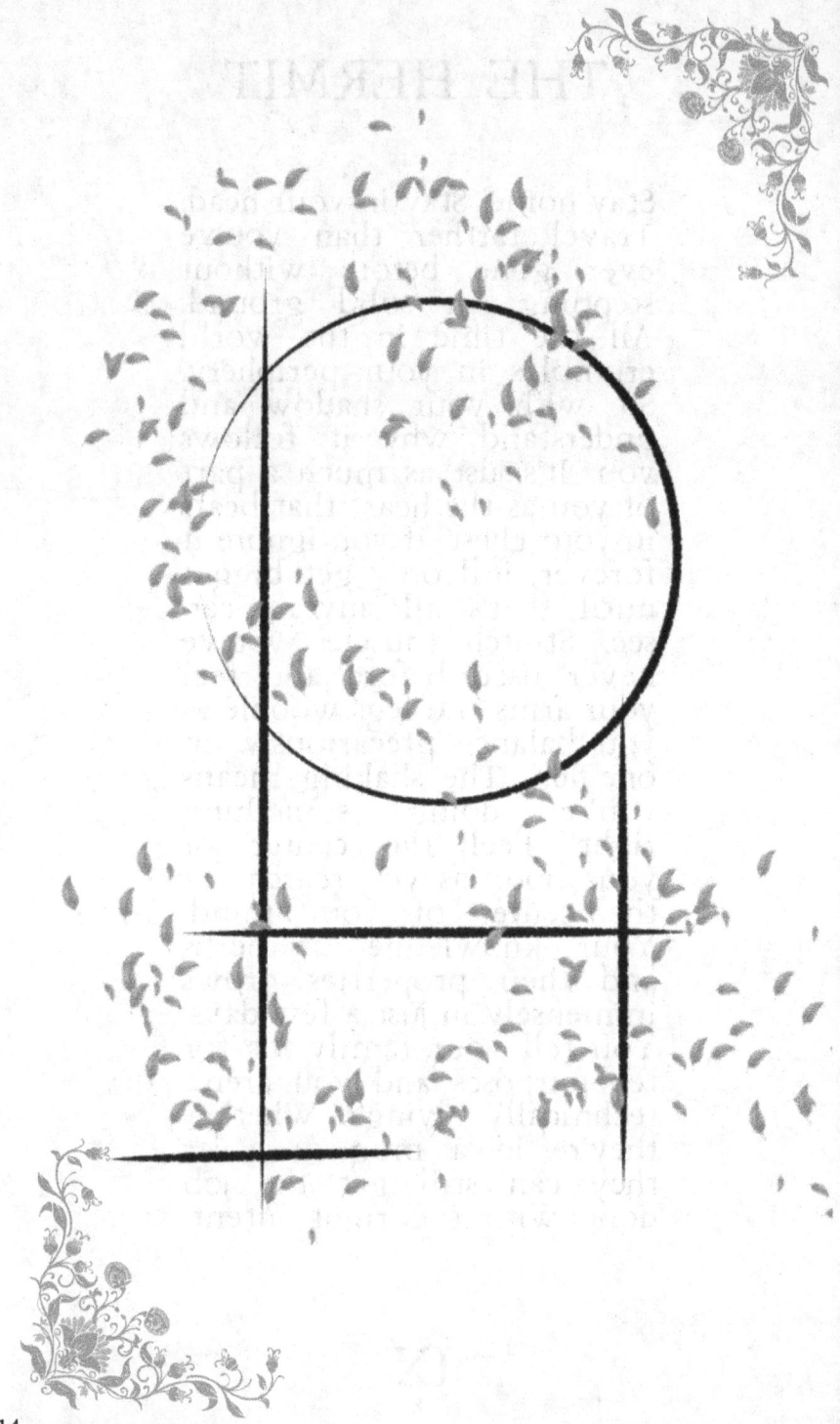

STRENGTH

I try to make my reflection stand tall, remind it not to curl inward anymore. I want to believe I'm ready to march out into the world. To be confident in my foliage and the solidity of my branches but, what if someone notices? What if people can tell that I've been tampered with, that some of my growth has shriveled and snapped off my branches. They see the glowing embers that I haven't been able to put out and their eyes look to mine with that soft gaze no one ever wants aimed in their direction. It doesn't matter how long it's been or how much I've healed. It will always be a part of my past, something I never wanted to define me. A stern gaze reflects back to me. *That isn't the only thing that defines who you are.* My hands clench at my sides. I recite until I feel them relax once more. I am a good listener. I can be funny on occasion. I am compassionate. I am a loyal friend. Small sprouts only just unfurling, but it's something I can work with.

VIII

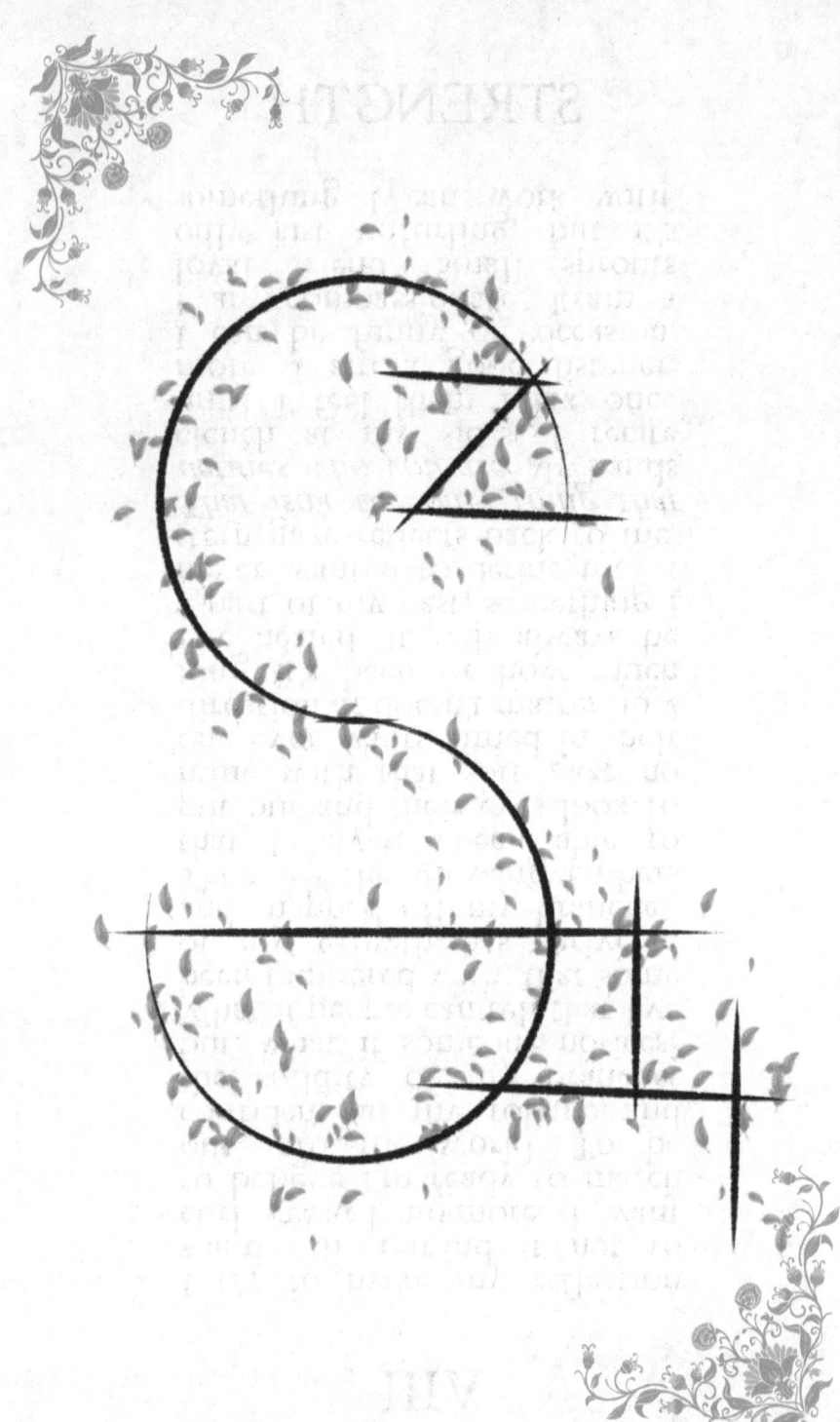

THE HANGED MAN

Strangers engulfed my vision until an old friend found me. I latched my talons onto her and followed wherever she went. She introduced me to the first people I called friends in this unfamiliar world. Each one just as awkward, but in their own unique way. We form a band of outcasts that gets stronger as days go on. It seemed like nothing could destroy those roots. Then my tower crumbles. Dark clouds cover the rays I once basked in. The roots turn to ash by someone who helped build them. I try to mend what's been broken. Smile as I'm exchanged with the match that lit the flame. All the while hiding my charred pieces from the ones I thought cared. When I start coughing up ash I decide to fly to a new part of the forest. That old friend once again guides me to somewhere I could blossom. It comes with a price. Just as she did, I must cut ties to truly be free enough to bask in this sun.

XII

THE MOON

It's easy to lose your way in the dark. The ash piles up around me until I'm suffocating myself. It was your fault. You're making too big a deal out of it. You should've seen the signs. I should've felt his breath on my neck as we gathered for a picture, his lips glancing over my skin. I pushed them aside. He was my friend. I sink down farther. You don't deserve a new beginning. My branches twist into gnarled forms. I squeeze my body as small as it can go. It was my job to fix it. Bring our group back to the way it was. All I did was run away into the arms of new, exciting people. You broke the best thing you had. My nails break the skin on my palm. I push back. If they were the best people for me then why did they side with him? When my breath fluttered as fast as my phoenix's wings if I so much as thought he was near, they did nothing. I push the ash out of my face and breathe in fresh air. It feels foreign in my throat.

XVIII

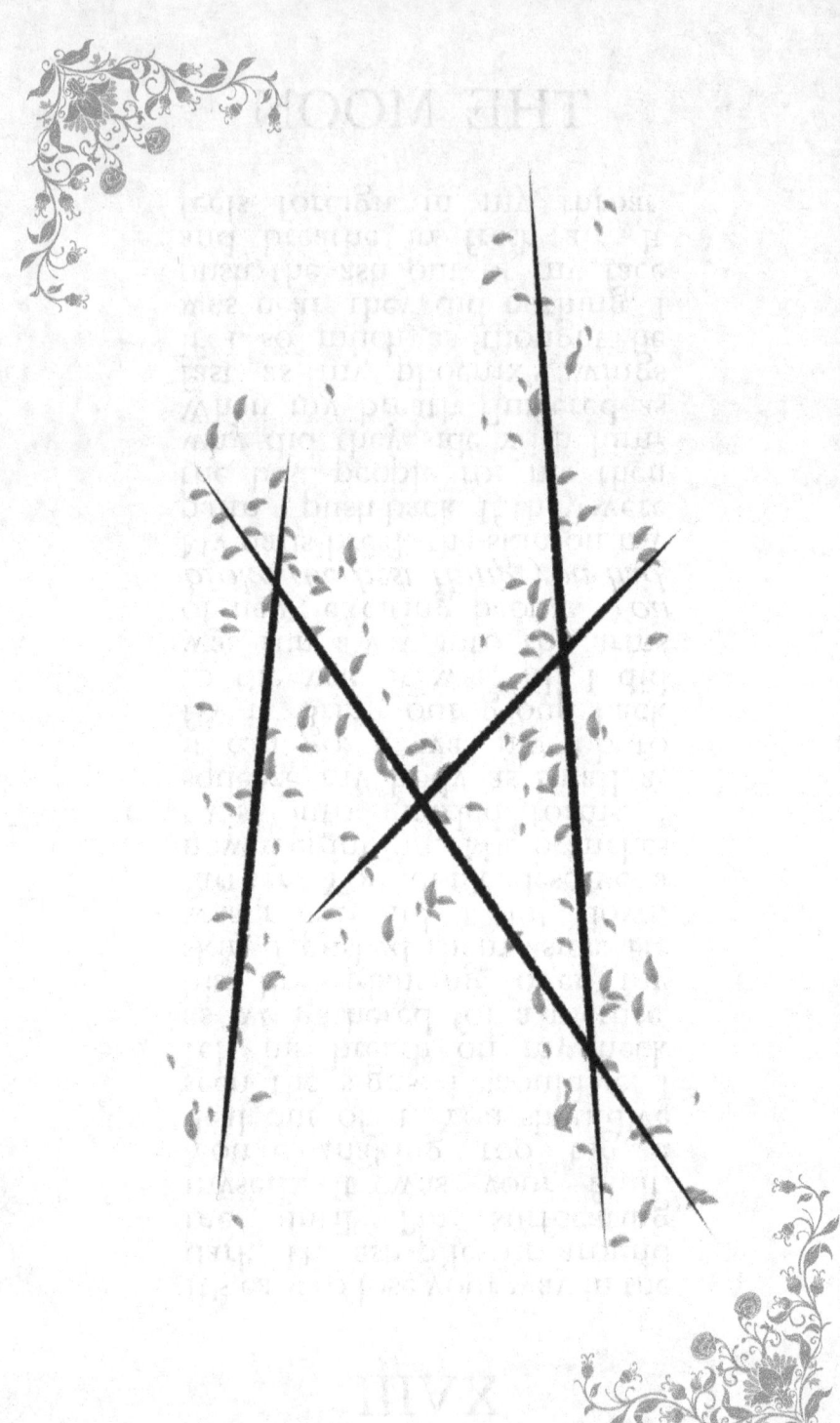

THE STAR

Breath in. My roots latch into Mother Nature. Breath out. I stretch my branches high, to almost touch the heavens above. Breath in. My mind begins to melt into the music, the vibrations resonating throughout my body. Breath out. I release my past and forgive myself. Breath in. The sweet, wooden smell of Nag Champa fills my lungs and suddenly I am lying in the bed of a forest. The trees that surround me stretch so high they seem to never end. I look pitiful in contrast, but I remind myself I have much more time to grow. Breath out. I can feel the energy fill me. A warm buzzing spreads from where my feet touch the Earth, a comforting reminder I'm not alone. Breath in. The shadow connected to me is something everyone has. As we strive for our happiness, so will there be struggles that come with it. Breath out. I feel myself being gently pulled back, the chime of renewal in my ear. Breath in. I release my past and forgive myself. My breath stutters.

XVII

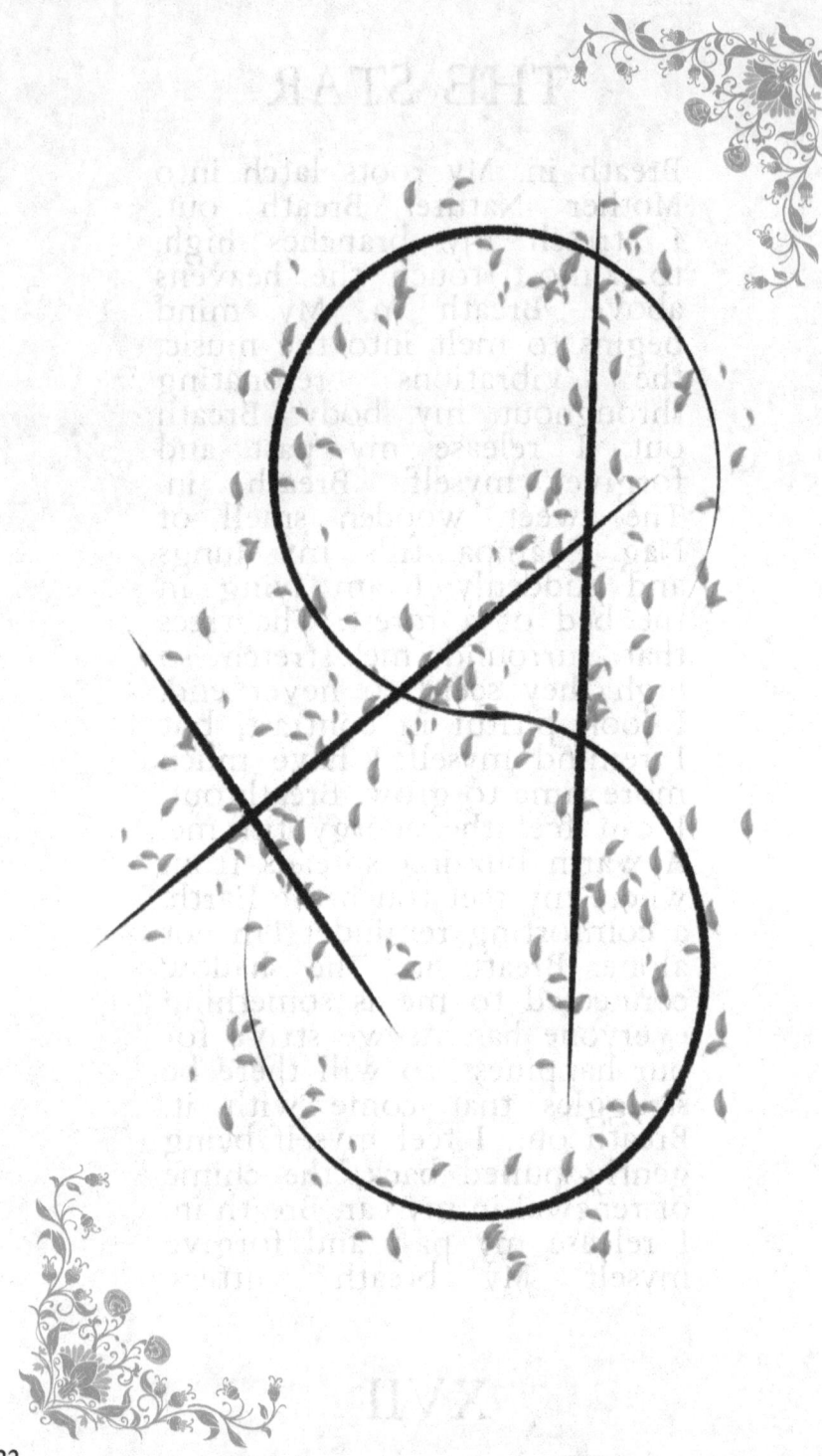

JUSTICE

XI

I don't blame myself anymore. It wasn't something I could control, no matter how desperately I wanted to. The circumstances were too messy for there to be a just end. Our group was knitted too tight for the brush to be sorted out clearly into right and wrong. I was burnt to ash by someone who didn't even remember lighting the fire. How were they to exile a close friend when all they knew was my truth and not his? No retribution, only compromise. We stayed separate until I could see him without more charred pieces flaking off me. Branches twisted and constricted my heart until all I could do was agree. They weren't to blame for a horror they didn't commit. As time went on, the branches grew tighter. Bitterness replaced my fear. I hid my burnt edges and extended one of my branches to try to bring normalcy for the sake of the others. When he snapped it, flames of my own making burnt the branches around my heart. I tore myself out of the brush, scrapes littered my bark, but I was free.

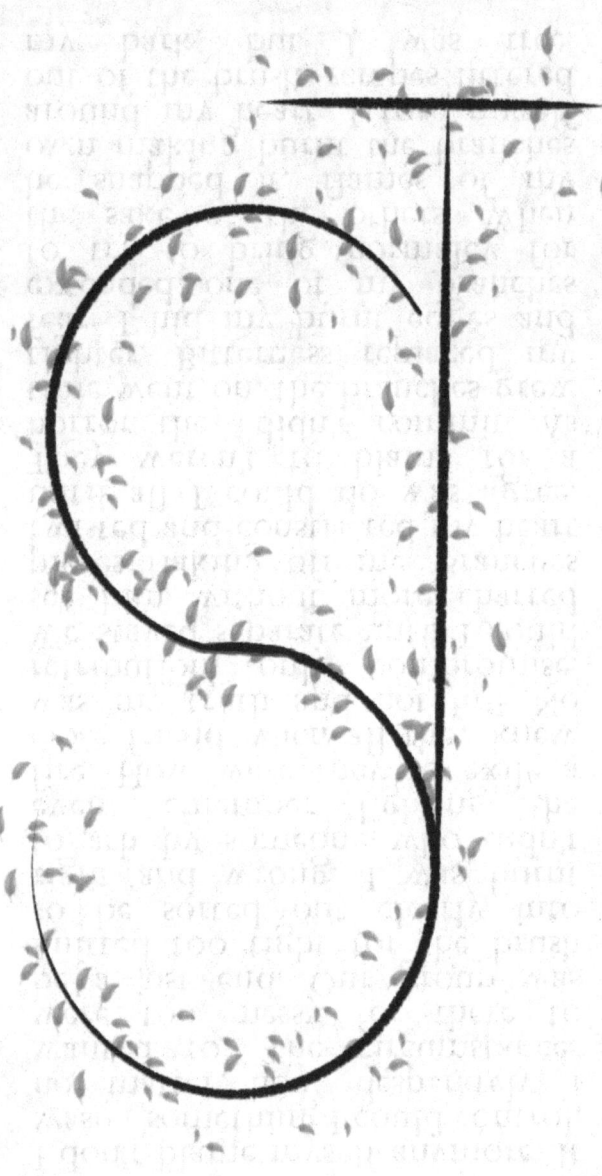

THE TOWER

I had once been flush with life. My branches had acorns and leaves abound. Ready to be reveled in by any wildlife that passed. My phoenix flew high, daring to meet the others that lived in the trees that surrounded me. I trusted them to land on my branches and enjoy my abundance. We were a family of strange personalities and similar journeys. They had done so much to help me believe I could take up space. Then one flew too close when I was curled in my nest. The caress of my back was like a match striking tinder. I was set ablaze. Sleek red feathers turned to flames before my eyes. Hot breath singed the hairs on my neck and the leaves I had cultivated crumbled to ashes floating high in the sky. All I could do was watch everything I nurtured deteriorate to charred remains. I gasped until my lungs were filled with smoke. My face wet from my eyes flushing out the ash, transfixed at the carnage before me.

XVI

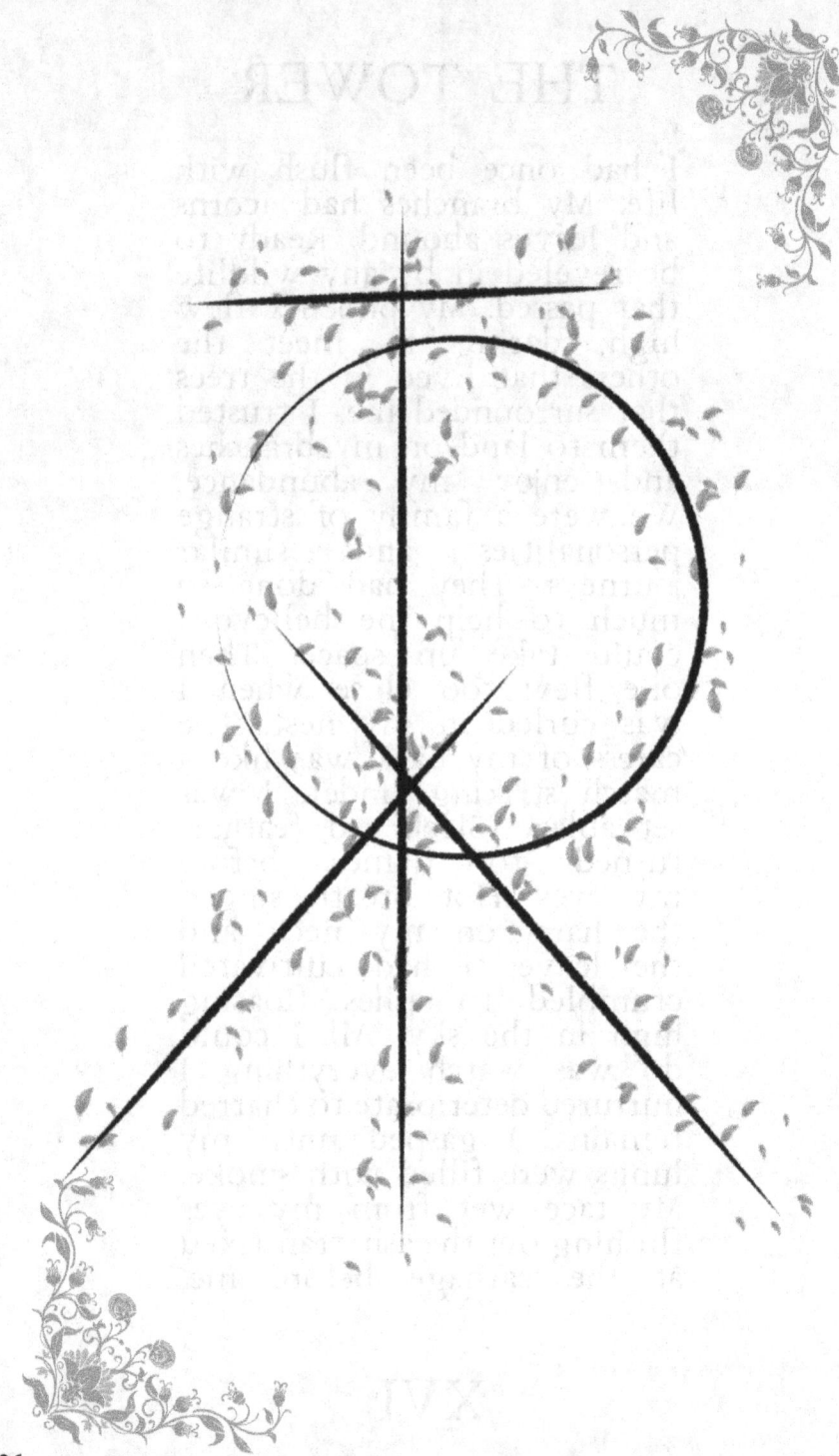

THE DEVIL

XV

My parents told me I would be judged for any sin I commit. I was told I would be sent to eternal damnation if I said a word people decided was bad. My brain spun with this knowledge, trying to make sense of it but it never clicked. The forced hand of my parents dragged me to service each week, not understanding why I felt like I was intruding. They said I could decide when I was older. The anger my father shows now when I tell him my decision begs to differ. I feel a hint of familiarity as I enter the threshold, but it flies off as quickly as it came. The time comes to take the body and I plant myself firmly to the bench, it isn't mine to take anymore. They are silent as they sit back down around me, accepting the small rebellion. My father still has a smile plastered on his face, believing I'll change my mind if I just sit here long enough. However, in my mind, there's no turning back. I've declined their lifelong offer of God in place of something I can control.

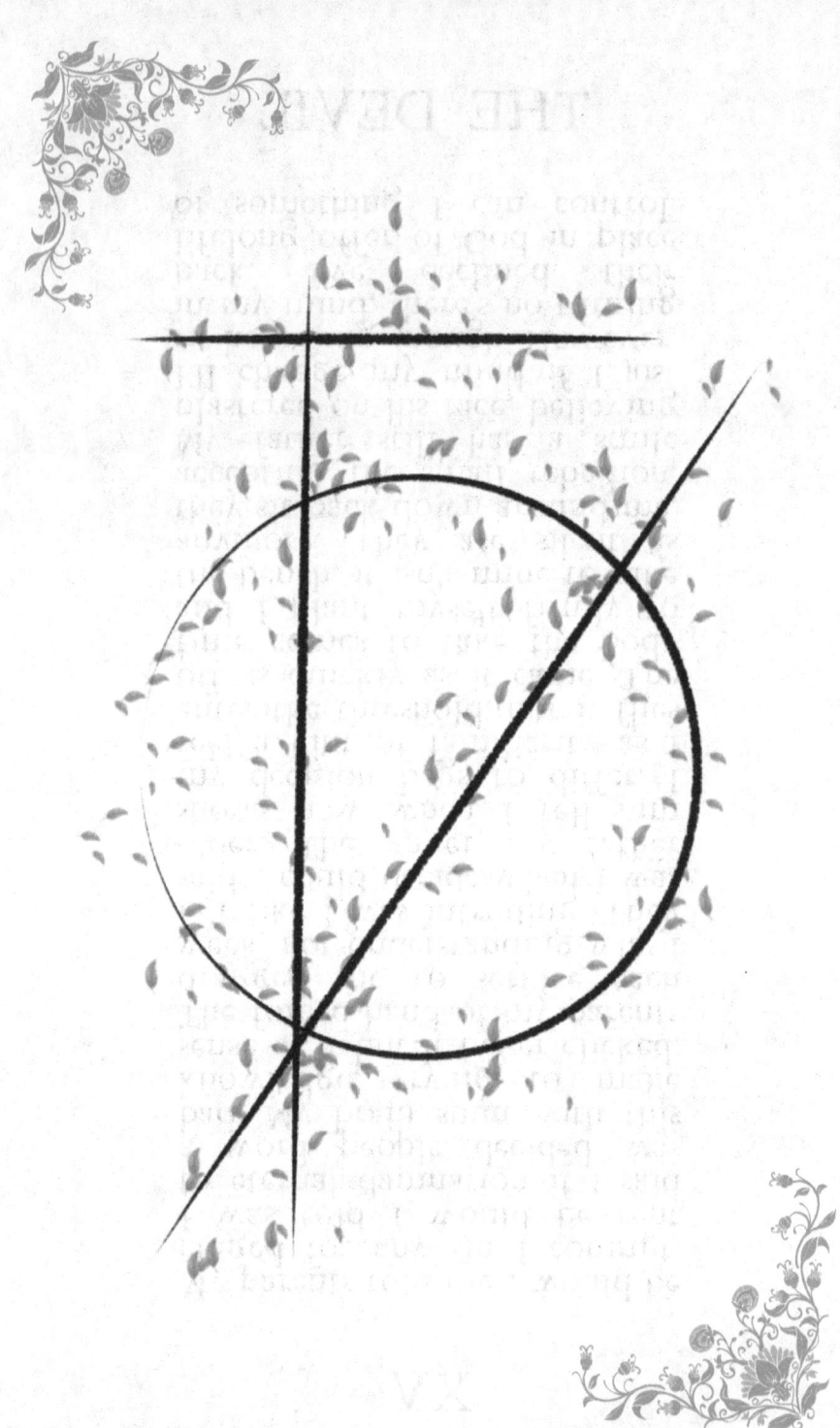

THE MAGICIAN

I take deep breaths, holding for just a moment before letting go. Murmurs echo from outside my door, I hear the birds sing as they fly from branch to branch. My roots plant into the floor as my mind reaches out in question. Energy flows through me that isn't mine and I send a wave of thanks. I gaze at the ingredients before me. My body buzzes with untapped energy. I go slow, putting careful thought and energy into each layer. Pink salt for healing. Lavender for peace. Rose petals for love. Honey for sweetness. A sigil of my manifestation. The energy spills out of my fingers after each piece. Collecting into the jar before me and mixing with the energy each piece holds. Pink wax drips from the candle I hold, dropping onto the corked jar. As it seals, so does my intent. I still once more and ground myself to the floor below, releasing the energy back into the Earth. As above, so below. As my word, so it is.

I

THE MAGICIAN

I awoke deep breaths, holding
for was a moment before
letting go. Munpora, echo
from outside my door. I hear
the birds sing as they fly from
branch to branch. My poets
plant into the floor as my
mind reaches for a question.
Energy flows through me,
singing praise aloud and a
prayer of thanks. I gaze at the
sphere here before me,
slightly bigger with untapped
energy to shape, perform
thought and merge
together in form. I imbue it
with power for peace,
love, light, for love. How to
harness. A puff of my
breath lit it up. I saw trees,
hills, oceans, mountains, all
in place, all along
presenting an arc in the
of the energy to shape,
holding it with me from
the candle I was dropping
onto the robes in tap. As it
took, so does my breath. I
am still once more and ground
myself to the floor below,
releasing the energy bred
into the earth as above, so
below. As my word, so it is.

JUDGEMENT

I am nothing. I am a blink of existence no one will miss. My eyes glaze over and drops fall down my face, leaving a wet trail behind. My hand grips my phone, the "regret to inform you" still shining brightly. My last chance of a new beginning torn away by my own hand. I'm too awkward. Too quiet. Too depressing. Too much nothing. Flames erupt inside me, but I can't let them destroy everything I've cobbled together. I need to release it. I take shaky steps to my desk and search until I find what I need. Its touch fills me with a sickening exhilaration. Before I give myself a second thought, I carve into one of my branches. It takes a few swipes before I see sap pouring out. It's bright like the flames I feel burning in me still. As the drop trickles down my bark, I feel a searing heat come from the wound and feel the flames in my chest ebb. In its place is a familiar numbness. I carefully wash and bandage myself before lying motionless on my bed.

XX

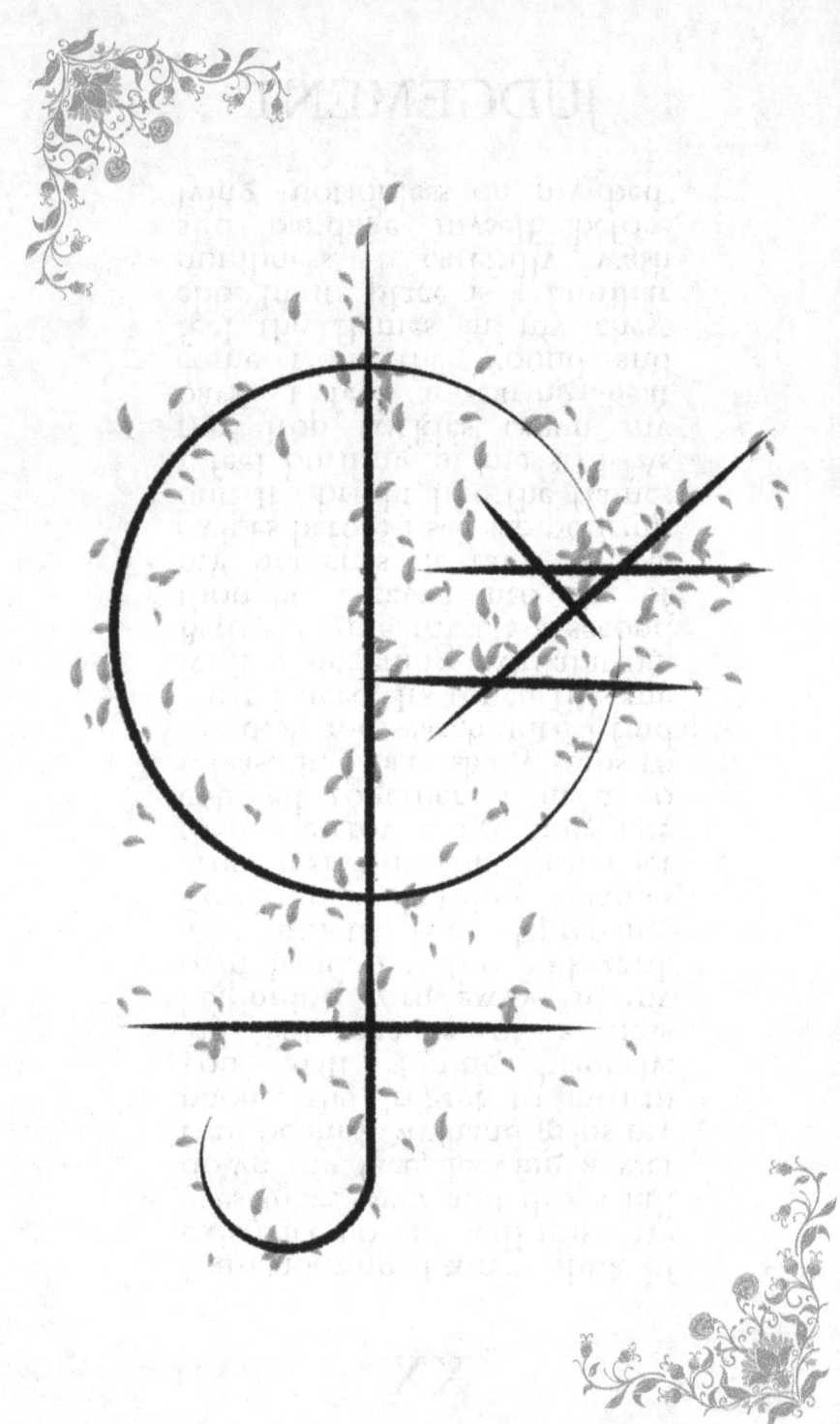

THE SUN

I'm surrounded, faces looking solely at me. They exude a light my oak yearns to reach into. My legs cross and uncross and my hand instinctively runs through my hair and pushes it all to the other side. I look around and see some familiar faces and slowly exhale. Then they ask the first question. "What could you contribute to the house?" My mind stalls and my mouth becomes a wasteland. The silence I've always known rings in my ear. The heat of their gaze flushes my face and all I can do is stare at the floor. I reach out for anything in my mind, but nothing seems good enough. I jolt when another voice speaks up. "What's your sign?" My body exhales as I answer the question easily. I fall into their welcoming nature and my body fills with a warmth it hasn't for a while. Not an uncontrollable burning that leaves everything in ashes, but the heat of the sun as you lie in the grass and it tickles at your face.

XIX

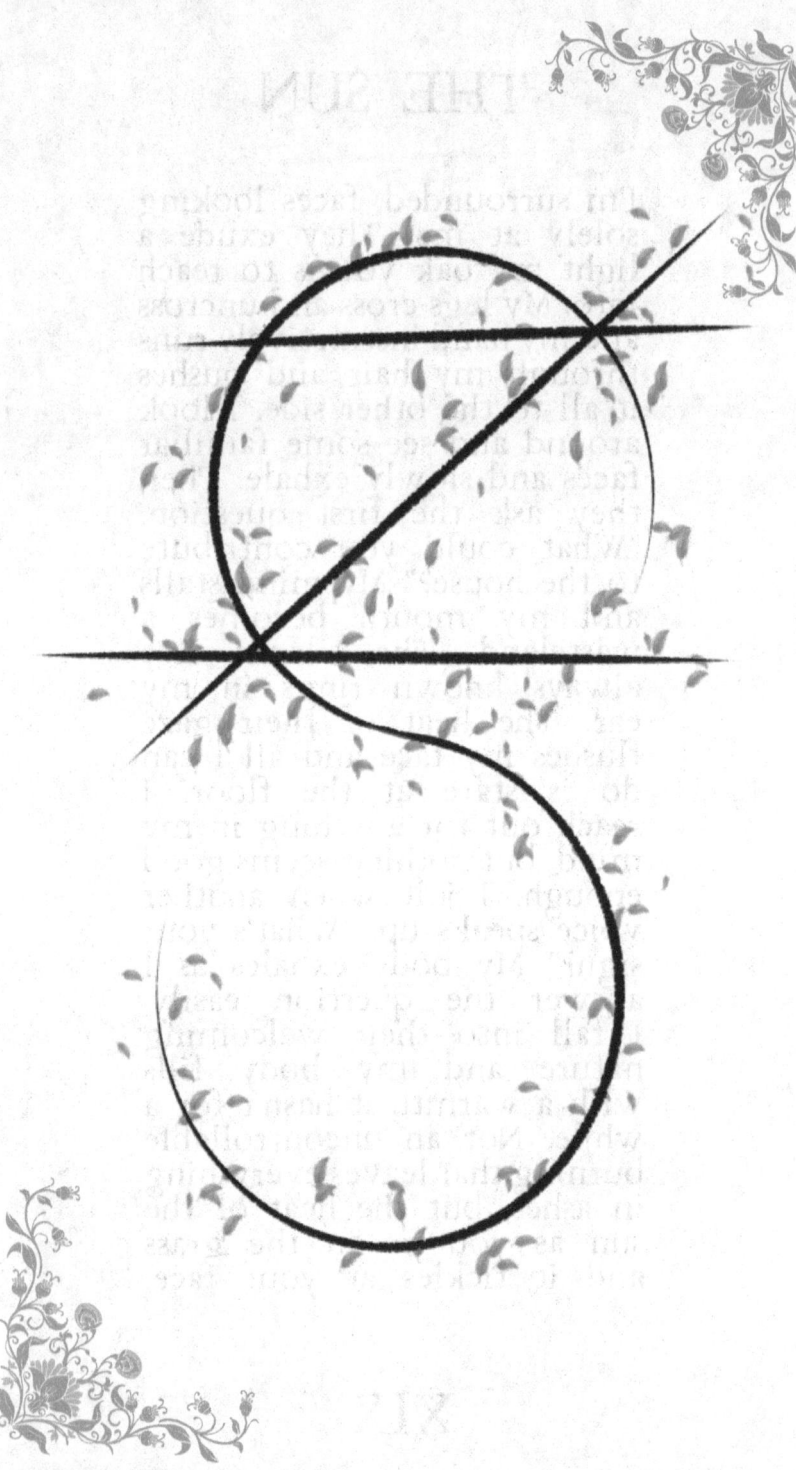

TEMPERANCE

My arms become scratched and splotches of purplish yellow blossom across my body. It's better down here, there are no surprises that can trick me into a false sense of security. My feet scrape across the ground. I can't seem to feel anything but the sting of my cuts. Then a strong wind blows, and I can feel my hatchling's wings spread behind me to take flight. I soar to the sky and a gentle warmth soothes the aches from the crash. But flying too high can be scary. The heat of the Sun sinks into my body and I want to absorb as much as I can before the next drop comes. I fly higher and higher before the heat sears my feathers. Suddenly, the wind rushes past me and I see the ground grow nearer. It would be easier to let it happen. Continue the cycle from high to low. But I remember the in-between. I remember the warmth radiating from the sun as the cool breeze flows past me. The calm. I open my wings against the force of the wind and the strain almost hurts as much as the fall. Almost.

XIV

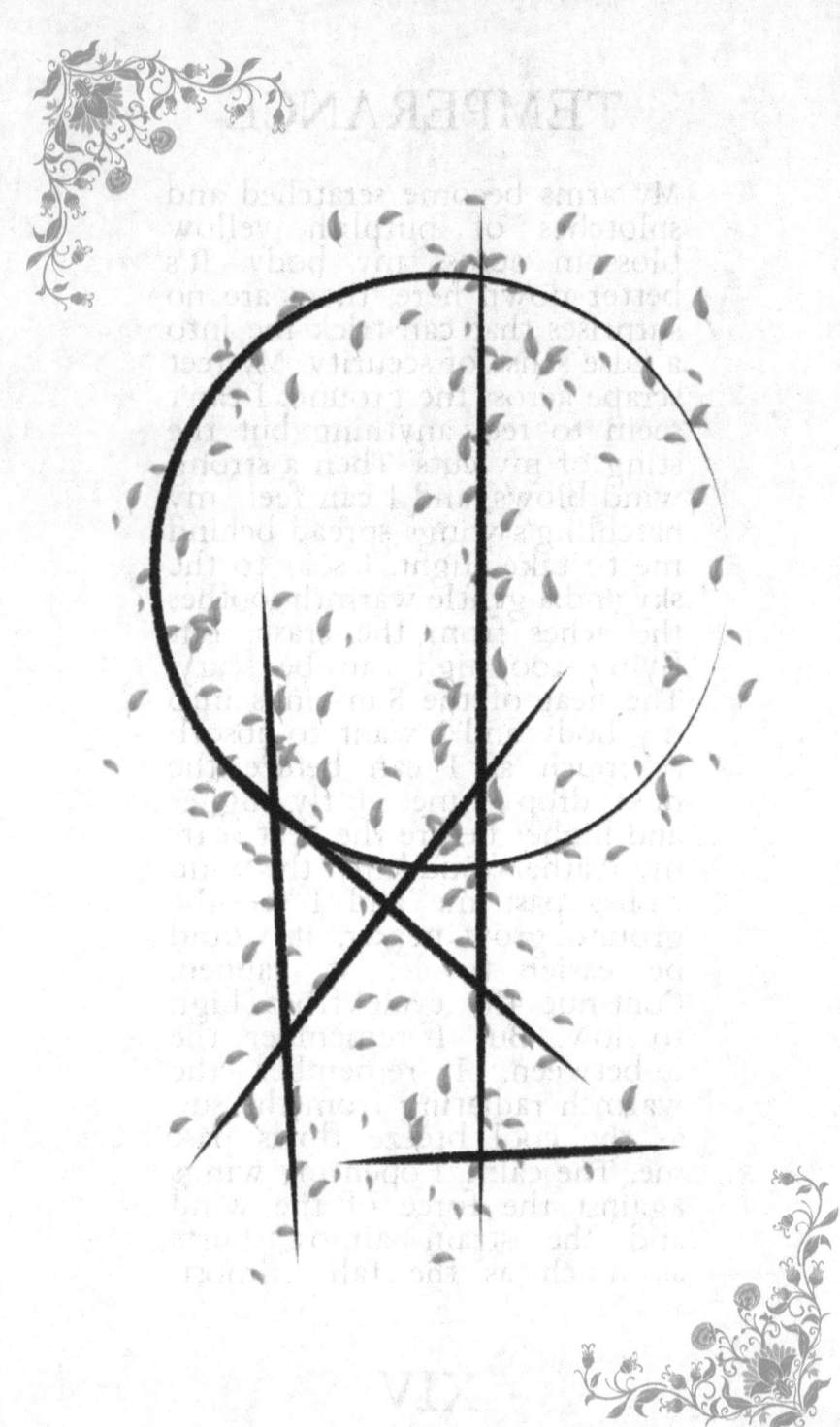

DEATH

His little princess. Her baby girl. Words I've heard all my life. Even as I jumped into the fray as my brothers tussled in the backyard, kicking and scratching my way to victory. When I vehemently refused to have anything to do with pink because it was 'girly'. A child with scratches on their arms and legs from trying to climb the tree the highest. It's a wonder they were shocked. Then again, they like to be blind to things they'd rather not deal with. A tether snapped when I finally told them. I had been set free from bending my branches to fit what they wanted to see. So, I thought. They smiled and nodded at my words, but every time they call me 'she' I'm reminded that an act is all it was. A gesture to keep me by their side. They tell me they'll always love me, but I wonder if that love is now lost with their little girl.

XIII

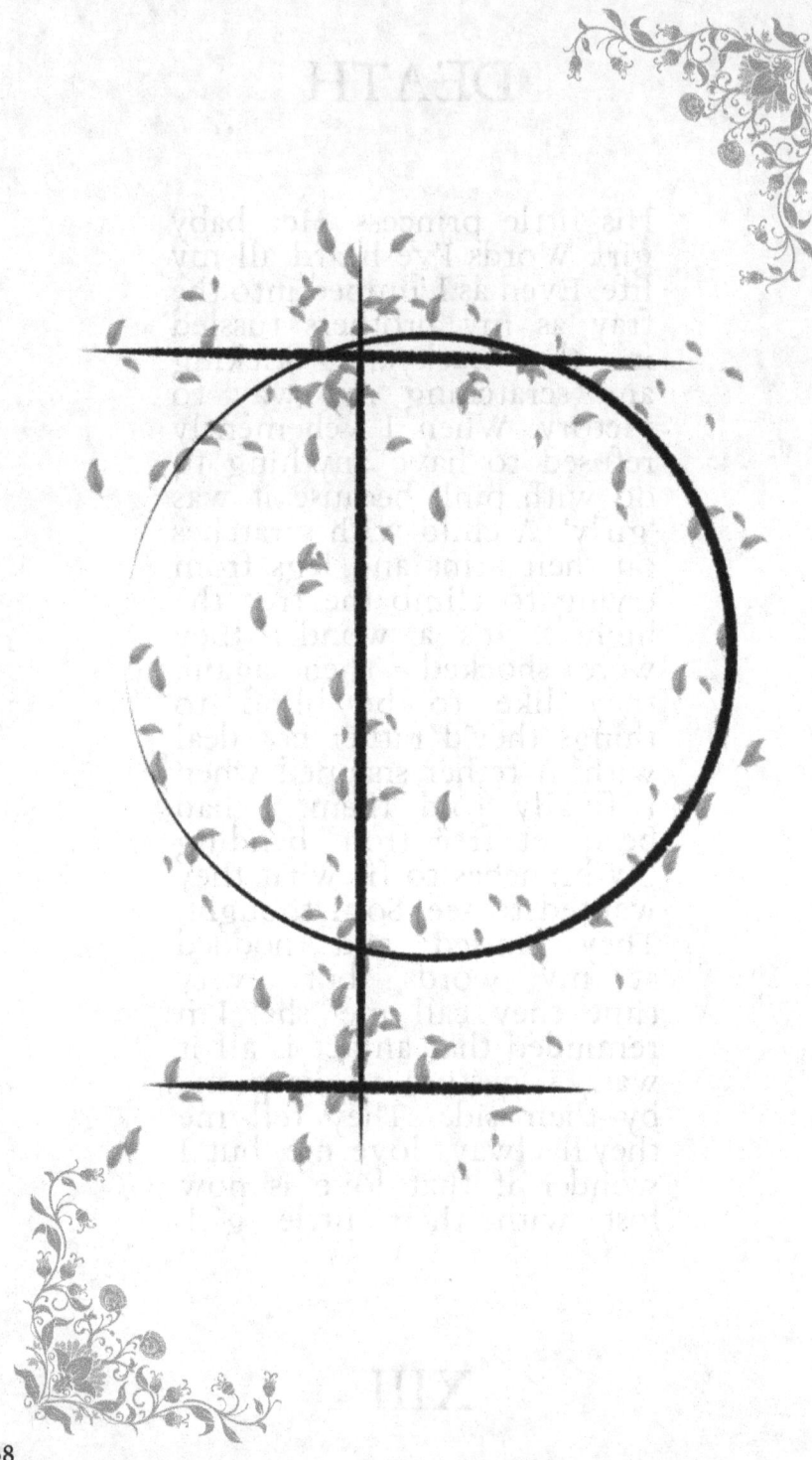

THE CHARIOT

It felt as if they were taking away the Sun. Something that had given me the chance to gain back any semblance of life. The house welcomed me with open arms, the various couches and tacked-up pictures giving it a homey feel. It was a shelter for any misfits who found themselves lost in the sea of strangers. The twisting stairways and creaky floorboards might frighten others with its heavy aura, but to me, it felt like a blanket encompassing me every time I entered. It took my petrified hatchling into its own nest while my charred remains healed from their destruction. I will never be able to repay it for my rejuvenation, they've made sure of that. They took our kindness as a point of attack and bore through its bark until they found a weakness. The reins I thought I had held were merely weeds grown to keep me in a fool's paradise. I've been pushed from the nest without a word of warning and am forced to fly away without the hope of a second glance.

VII

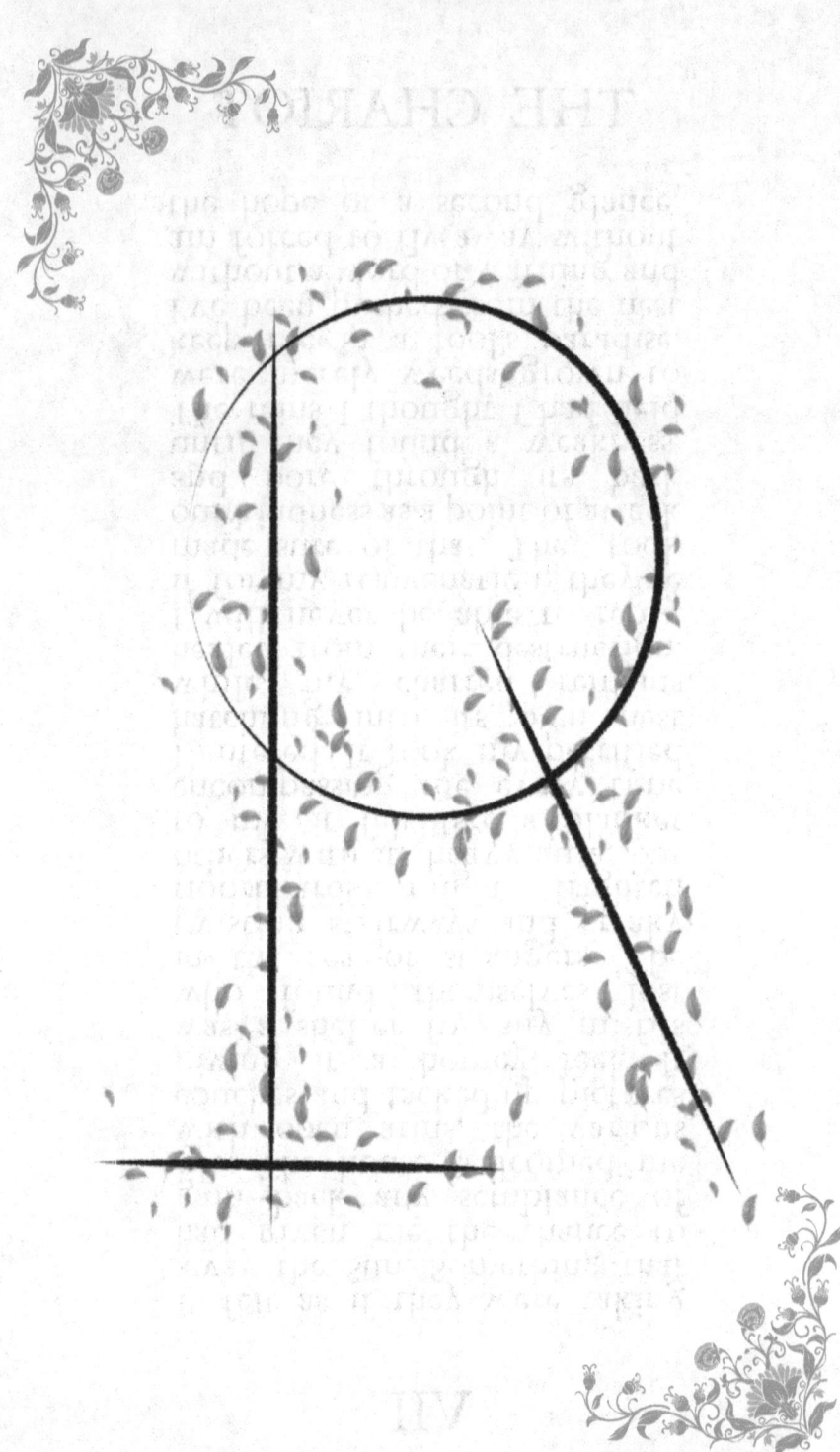

WHEEL OF FORTUNE

The wind blows across my face. My eyes close and I fall back on my arms. Life is cyclical. Fall turns to winter turns to spring turns to summer. Flowers grow, blossom, bask, if only for a moment, before losing their petals and succumbing to the cold. Only for it to happen once more. What goes up must come down. Who once was happy will fall to sadness. Maybe it isn't fair, but when has life ever been that? Just because the sun sets doesn't mean it won't rise. Just because my chest aches and I can't seem to leave my bed, doesn't mean it won't get better. Days will come where I will laugh so hard, I can't breathe, or watch as the rain pours outside, cuddled in a fuzzy blanket. There will be more days of emptiness, where I beat on my chest to try and make it thump again. Or when it all becomes too unbearable, and I just sit on my rug surrounded by used tissues until the room darkens. I breathe in the warm spring air and let this knowledge flow out of me. I'll take each season when it comes.

X

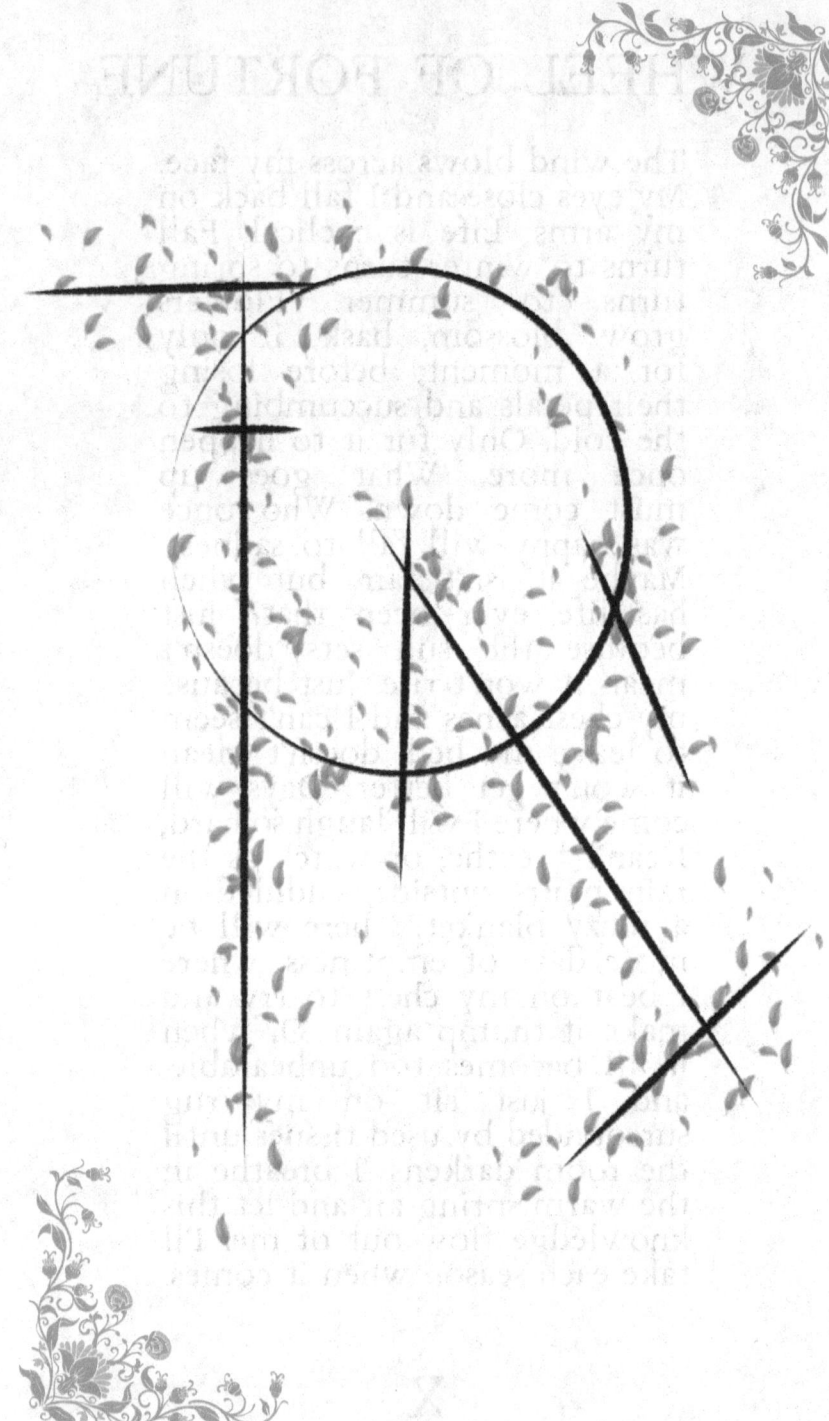

THE WORLD

The warmth of the mug heats my hands. The taste of chamomile and lavender fills my mouth, and my muscles relax as the heat spreads into my body. I'm curled up on my bed watching some stupid show that I'm barely paying attention to. My mind falls back onto all the things I'm putting off for this droplet of peace. There are jobs I need to apply to, burns I still must heal, and a shadow that continues to loom behind me. The work never ends. Every time I feel like I'm close, more root rot shows itself. It might take me until my face wrinkles and my hair turns gray. I don't think that means it isn't worth it. I shouldn't put down the story before I reach the conclusion. I don't want to rush and miss out on a moment that could have been a defining part of who I am to become. Laughter bursts from my laptop and I focus on the scene in front of me. Someone else's life has my attention for once. My journey isn't over.

XXI

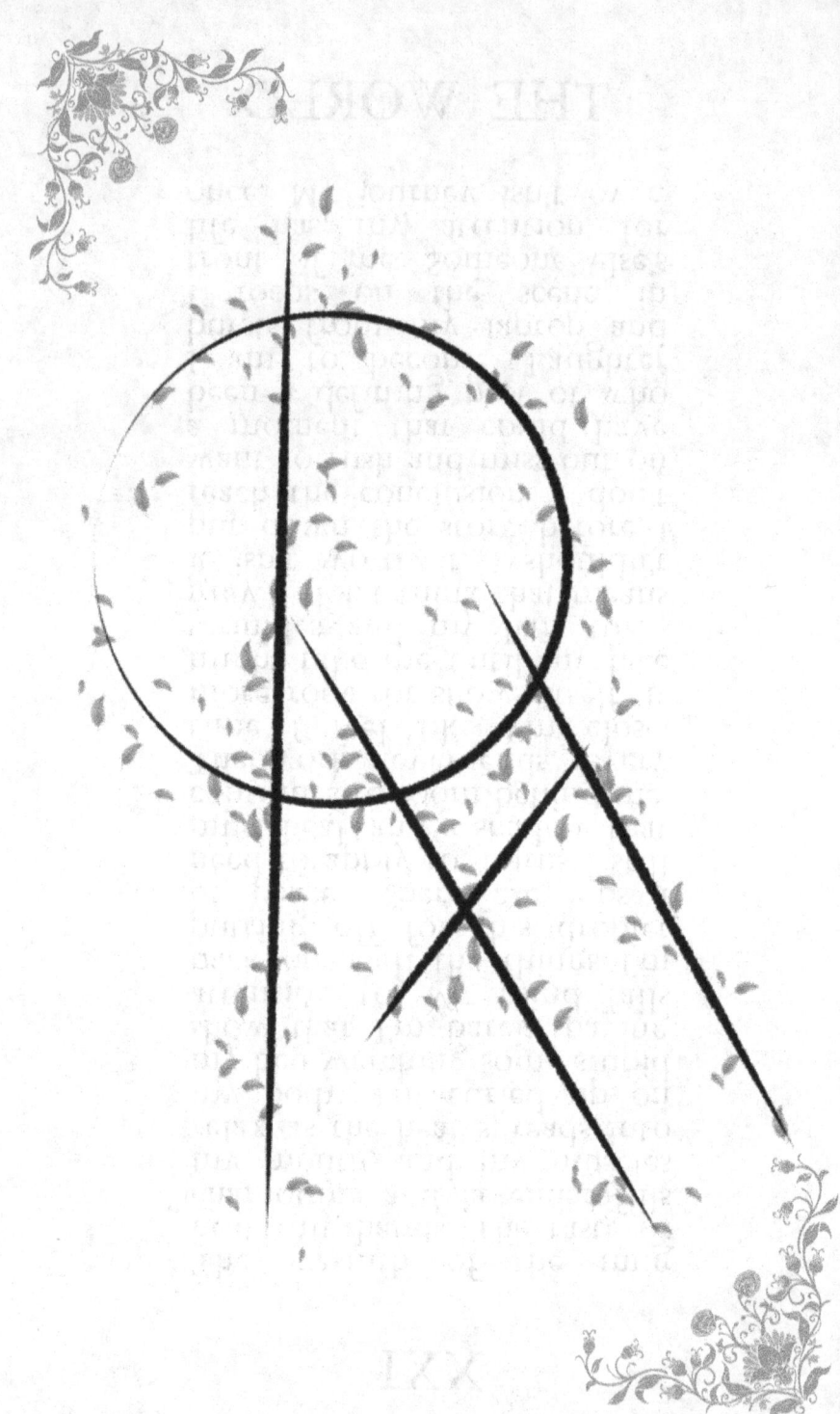

Acknowledgements

Thank you to the entire family of Ia'ana, without you, I wouldn't be where I am today. My first step to becoming myself came from you, and you continually supported, encouraged, and helped me. I ael-like it is impossible to repay you, hopefully, one day I'll be able to. <3

Thank you to my friends who have always supported me, even when I felt I didn't deserve it. Even if we aren't as close as we were in college, I'll always love you, and my door is open if you ever need it.

Acknowledgements

Thank you to the community of Framar, without you, I would not be where I am today. My first step to becoming my best self came from you, and you continually supported, encouraged, and helped me. I feel like it's impossible to repay you. Hopefully, one day I'll be able to. <3

Thank you to my friends who have always supported me, even when I felt I didn't deserve it. Even if we aren't as close as we were in college, I'll always love you guys! My door's open if you ever need it.

Thank you to my poetry Professor, who fueled my fiery passion for poetry (even if she didn't know it), and my classmates who had to read this back when it was only a ghost of what it is now. Thank you for bearing with me and my first drafts!

And thank you to the one who was there through it all. Who saw me at my worst and pushed me to believe in myself and my poetry. I wish you the best.

About the Author

Luck Zytowski is a queer witch and author who prefers to sit in a forest to crowds. 'MAJOR' is their first self-publication, which combines their love of poetry with their craft. When they aren't writing, you can find them singing and dancing badly at their home in Virginia.

www.ingramcontent.com/pod-product-compliance
Lightning Source LLC
Chambersburg PA
CBHW011151290426
44109CB00025B/2577